LET'S CELEBRATE PASSOVER

Contents

Music production and recording by *Gary Schreiner*
Cover created by *Julie Philips*
Book design & illustrations by *Barbara Hoag Helgesen*
Drum programming by *Jim Mussen*
Performers: *Laura Donaldson, Gabe Lubin, Arthur Purvis, Marisa Stewart, Karen Schwartz*
Follow, Follow Me sung by *Catherine Russell*
Clarinet: *Paul Shapiro*
Guitar: *Paul Livant*

Created by *Elissa Oppenheim Schreiner and Sunnie Miller*
Produced by *Elissa Oppenheim Schreiner*
Story dialogue and book by *Judith Weinstein*
Lyrics by *Sunnie Miller*
Music composed and arranged by *Elissa Oppenheim Schreiner*
Dialogue performed by *Neva Small*

ASTOR BOOKS

What Does It Mean?

AFIKOMEN: The name given to the middle one of the three matzohs on the Seder plate. Often a piece of this is hidden, and the children search for it after the Seder.

ELIJAH: A prophet of Israel who is said to appear on the eve of Passover. A glass of wine is on the Seder table, awaiting his arrival.

FOUR QUESTIONS: The youngest at the Seder table recites these from the Haggadah.

HAGGADAH: The story of the Exodus from Egypt which is read at the Passover Seder.

KNEIDLACH: Matzoh meal dumplings.

KREMSLACH: Matzoh meal pancakes.

MATZOH: Unleavened (unrisen) bread eaten during the seven days of Passover.

PESACH: Another way of saying "Passover," which begins on the 15th day of Nisan and lasts for seven days. It celebrates the Hebrew Exodus from Egypt and the protection that God gave to the Jews when the angel of death "passed over" their houses.

SEDER: The Passover holiday meal.

The Seder

Helping to set the table is a good way to prepare for Passover. One plate is put in front of the leader, and it is called the Seder plate. The following are arranged on the plate:

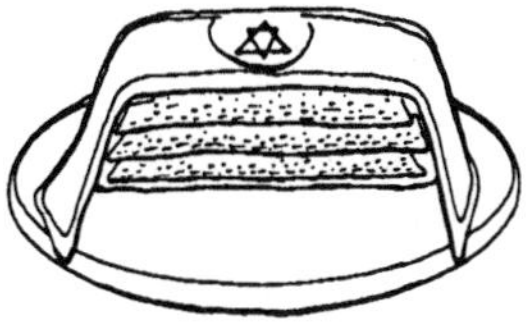

MATZOH
Three pieces

CHAROSET
A mixture of fruit, nuts, grape juice and spices symbolizing the mortar (cement) which our ancestors used when they were slaves.

BEITSAH
A roasted egg symbolizing life.

MAROR
Bitter herbs or horseradish root representing the bitter lives of our ancestors.

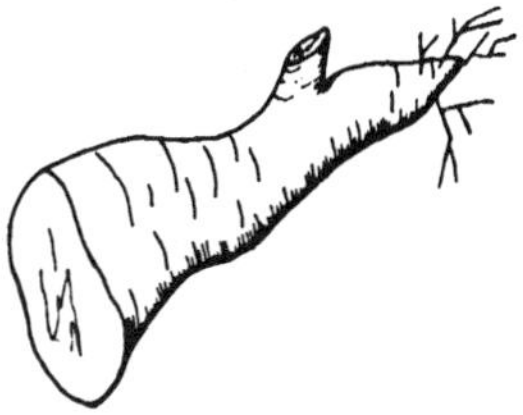

KARPAS
The parsley or green herb representing springtime and hope.

ZEROA
A roasted shank bone representing the ancient Passover sacrifice.

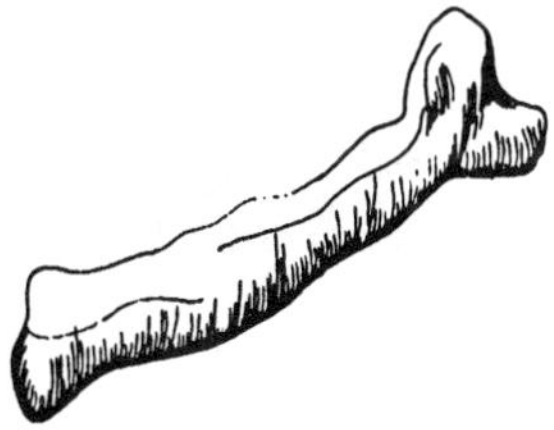

Adults and children say the blessing over the Matzoh:

Blessed is the Lord our God, Ruler of the universe,
Who brings forth bread from the earth.

Ba-ruch a-ta, A-do-nai E-lo-hei-nu, me-lech ha-o-lam,
ha-mo-tsi le-chem min ha-a-rets.

Passover Treats

Always ask an adult to help you when cooking.

Charoset

This recipe is for 6-8 people and is placed on the Seder table.

INGREDIENTS	UTENSILS
1 tart apple	apple peeler
1/4 cup chopped walnuts	knife
1/4 teaspoon cinnamon	chopper
1/4 teaspoon ginger	measuring spoons
1/4 teaspoon nutmeg	mixing bowl
2 tablespoons grape juice	spatula

Peel, core and chop the apple.
Chop the walnuts.
Add the apple and walnuts to the rest of the ingredients.
Mix well and put into a pretty serving dish.

ENJOY!

Matzoh Pancakes

This recipe makes approximately 12-15 pancakes.

INGREDIENTS	UTENSILS
3 eggs	2 bowls
1/2 cup matzoh meal	measuring cups
1/2 cup water	measuring spoons
1/2 teaspoon salt	beater or blender
oil for frying	frying pan
	spatula
	tablespoon

Cover bottom of frying pan with oil and pre-heat.
Separate the yolks from the egg whites. Put into two bowls.
Beat the egg whites until they are white and fluffy.
Mix the egg yolks with the matzoh meal and slowly add the water. Add the salt. Mix well.
Blend the beaten egg whites with the egg yolk mixture.
Mix well.
Using the tablespoon, spoon the pancake mixture into the hot oil.
Fry on both sides until brown.
Drain on paper towels.
Serve with sugar or jam.

Passover Fun

Quiz:

Perhaps the one answering the most questions correctly can win a prize!

1. What does "Passover" mean?
2. Who led the Jews out of Egypt?
3. Why do we eat Matzoh on Passover?
4. Why do we eat bitter herbs at the Seder?
5. Why do we dip food into salt water?

Answers on page 15

Search & Find Puzzle

H	O	A	R	A	H	P	E
A	E	D	R	J	H	A	L
G	G	M	O	S	E	S	I
G	Y	L	C	U	R	S	J
A	P	N	Y	T	B	O	A
D	T	Q	Z	M	S	V	H
A	F	I	K	O	M	E	N
H	X	S	E	D	E	R	T

Answers on page 15

Study the words listed, then study the diagram. The words in the diagram will always be in a line (read up or down, left to right, right to left or even on a diagonal). Draw a circle around the words you find. Letters may be used in more than one word, and there will be unused letters left in the diagram.

HAGGADAH • EGYPT • MOSES
HERBS • PASSOVER • ELIJAH
SEDER • AFIKOMEN • PHARAOH

Crossword Puzzle

Across

2. What we search for after our Passover dinner.
4. The place from which the Jews fled during the Exodus.
5. We dip our food into water containing this.
6. Name for a special Passover dinner.
8. What we eat instead of bread.
10. A mixture of fruit, nuts, juice and spices.
14. Salt water is a symbol of the _____ shed by our ancestors in slavery.
15. Passover is celebrated on the 15th ___ of Nisan.

Down

1. The name for the story of the Exodus, which is read during Passover.
3. The man who led the Exodus.
7. Horseradish ____ represents the bitter lives of our ancestors.
9. Passover is a special _________ for Jewish people.
11. Bitter _____ are placed on the Seder plate.
12. We also place a roasted ____ on the Seder plate.
13. The angel of death passed over the houses of the ________ people.

Answers on page 15

THE AFIKOMEN MYSTERY

Music by Elissa Oppenheim Schreiner
Lyric by Sunnie Miller

THE FOUR QUESTIONS
(Ma Nishtana)

Traditional

Additional music by Elissa Oppenheim Schreiner
Additional lyric by Sunnie Miller
Arranged by Elissa Oppenheim Schreiner

Why is this night of Passover different from all other nights of the year? On all other nights, we eat bread or matzoh. Why on this night, do we eat only matzoh?

On all other nights, we eat all kinds of vegetables and herbs. Why do we eat maror tonight?

On all other nights, we never dip herbs in salt water or anything else. Why do we dip the parsley in salt water and the bitter herbs in charoset tonight?

On all other nights, everyone may sit upright or recline at the table. Why do we all recline tonight?

Additional Verse

4. She-b'hol ha-lë-lot a-nu oh-lin bën yosh-vin u-vën
m'su-bin, bën yosh-vin u-vën m'su-bin, ha-
lai-la ha-ze, ha-lai-la ha-ze ku-la-nu m'su-bin,
ha-lai-la ha-ze, ha-lai-la ha-ze ku-la-nu m'su-bin.

AVADIM HAYINU

Traditional

Additional music by Elissa Oppenheim Schreiner
Additional lyric by Sunnie Miller

IT'S THE WAY IT'S GOTTA BE

Music by Elissa Oppenheim Schreiner
Lyric by Sunnie Miller

FOUR KINDS OF CHILDREN

(The Child Who Asks Questions, the Shy Child, the Angry Child, the Young Child)

Music by Elissa Oppenheim Schreiner
Lyric by Sunnie Miller

Lively, Latin feel

WHO KNOWS ONE?
(Echad Mi Yodea)

Traditional

Music arranged by Elissa Oppenheim Schreiner
Lyric adapted by Sunnie Miller

FOLLOW, FOLLOW ME

Music by Elissa Oppenheim Schreiner
Lyric by Sunnie Miller

DAYENU

Traditional

Music arranged by Elissa Oppenheim Schreiner

Additional Verses

4. Had he cared for us in the desert,
   And not helped us for forty years,
   That would have been enough,
   Dayënu.

5. Had he helped us for forty years
   And not fed us with the Mana
   That would have been enough,
   Dayënu.

6. Had he fed us with the Mana,
   And not given us the Sabbath,
   That would have been enough,
   Dayënu.

7. Had he given us the Sabbath,
   And not brought us to Mount Sinai,
   That would have been enough,
   Dayënu.

8. Had he brought us to Mount Sinai,
   And not given us the Torah,
   That would have been enough,
   Dayënu.

9. Had he given us the Torah,
   And not led us to Is-ra-el-
   That would have been enough,
   Dayënu.